DANGEROUSLY

DIRTY

DAD

JOKES

What do you call a herd of masturbating cows?

Beef strokin' off.

How is life like toilet paper?

Either you're on a roll or you're getting shit on.

Why do mermaids wear seashells?

Because B-shells are too small.

What did the leper tell the prostitute?

Keep the tip.

What did one ass cheek say to the other ass cheek?

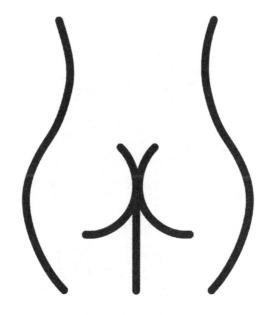

Together we can stop this shit.

What do you
do when your
cat dies?

Play with your
neighbor's pussy
instead.

How do you make a pool table laugh?

Tickle its balls.

Did you hear about the constipated accountant?

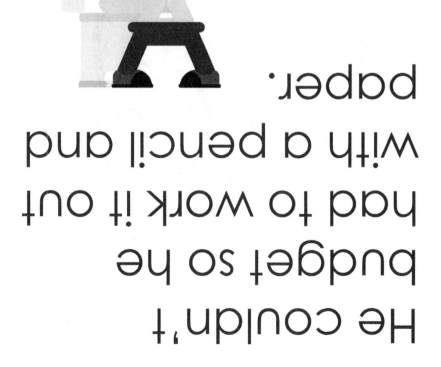

He couldn't budget so he had to work it out with a pencil and paper.

What do you call a cheap circumcision?

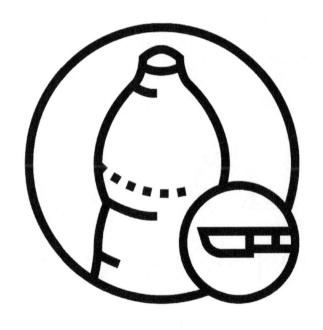

A rip-off.

What is the difference between a tire and 365 used condoms?

One is a Goodyear and the other is a great year.

How is sex like a game of Euchre?

You don't need a partner if you have a good hand.

What is Moby Dick's dad's name?

Papa Boner.

Why isn't there a pregnant Barbie doll?

Ken came in another box.

What do you call the lesbian version of a cock block?

A beaver dam.

What do a
Rubik's cube
and a penis
have in
common?

They get harder
the more you
play with them.

What do you get when you jingle Santa's balls?

A white Christmas.

What do you call an expert fisherman?

A master baiter.

What do you get when you cross a dick with a potato?

A dictator.

Why can't you hear rabbits bangin'?

Because they have cotton balls.

What is the
difference
between a
pickpocket and
a peeping tom?

One snatches
your watch, the
other watches
your snatch.

What do a nearsighted gynecologist and a puppy have in common?

A wet nose.

How do you make your wife scream during sex?

Call her and tell her about it.

What is the difference between hungry and horny?

Where you stick the cucumber.

What goes in hard and dry but comes out soft and wet?

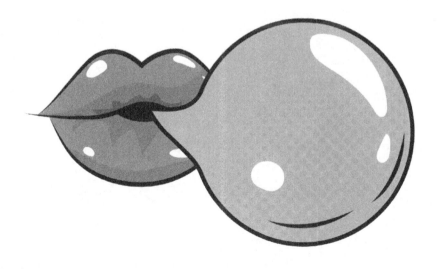

Chewing gum.

What is the difference between your penis and a bonus check?

Someone is always willing to blow your bonus check.

What did the sign at the out-of-business brothel say?

Beat it, we're closed.

What did one
saggy boob say
to the other
saggy boob?

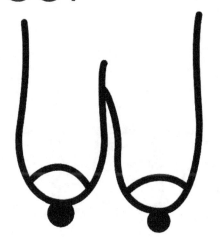

If we don't get
some support,
people will think
we're nuts.

What did the penis say to the condom?

Cover me, I'm goin' in.

What is the difference between a golf ball and a G-spot?

A man will actually try to find a golf ball.

What did the elephant say to the naked man?

How do you breathe out of that thing?

What do you do if your wife starts smoking?

Slow down and use some lubricant.

What is 6 inches long, 2 inches wide, and makes everyone go crazy?

$100 bill.

How do you spot a blind man at a nude beach?

It's not hard.

What does a horny frog say?

Rub it rub it.

What did the clitoris say to the vulva?

It's all good in the hood.

Why is masturbation the same as procrastination?

It's feels good until you realize you're fucking yourself.

Why did the dick go crazy?

Someone was messing with its head.

What does Popeye use for lube?

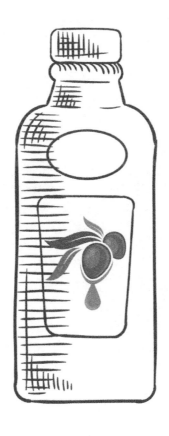

Olive Oyl.

Why is Santa's sack so big?

He only comes
once a year.

What is the difference between a pregnant lady and a lightbulb?

You can unscrew a lightbulb.

What is better than pansies on your piano?

Tulips on your organ.

What is the speed limit in bed?

68 because once you hit 69 you have to turn around.

Why do walruses love Tupperware parties?

Because they're always on the lookout for a tight seal.

How is being in the military like getting a blow job?

The closer you get to discharge, the better it feels.

Why was Tigger in the bathroom for so long?

He had Pooh stuck inside him.

Have you ever had sex while camping?

It's fucking intense.

What did the guy say when he was caught masturbating to an optical illusion?

It's not what it looks like!

What is a horny pirate's worst nightmare?

A sunken chest and no booty.

What is the difference between a snowman and a snowwoman?

Snowballs.

When should condoms be used?

In every conceivable occasion.

How is sex like air?

It's not a big deal until you aren't getting any.

What are the bestselling Disney toys?

Woody and Buzz.

What does a man need after a long day?

Oral support.

What do you call
a guy with a small
dick?

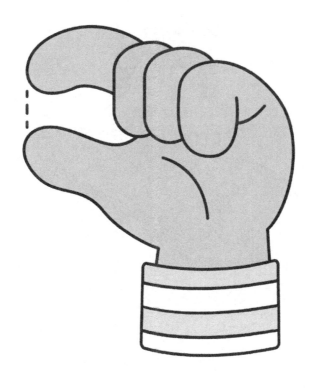

Justin.

Why was the guitar teacher fired?

For fingering a minor.

Want to hear a joke about my pussy?

Never mind, you'll never get it.

What did Cinderella do when she got to the ball?

Made choking noises.

Who can make more money, a drug dealer or a prostitute?

A prostitute because she can wash her crack and resell it.

What is the difference between your job and your wife?

After 5 years your job will still suck.

What is the
difference
between your
dog and your
wife?

Your dog will
come when its
told.

What do tofu and dildos have in common?

They are both meat substitutes.

What is the difference between a Greyhound terminal and a lobster with boobs?

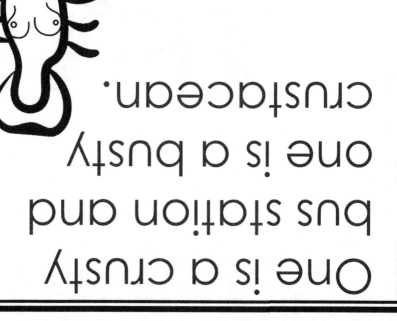

One is a crusty bus station and one is a busty crustacean.

Did you see that man without a penis?

He came out of nowhere.

What is the difference between oral and anal sex?

One makes your whole week and the other makes your hole weak.

What do you call 2 lesbians in a closet?

A liquor cabinet.

What do you get when you cross a rooster with an owl?

A cock that stays up all night.

How is virginity like a soap bubble?

One prick and it's gone.

What is the difference between a chickpea and a garbanzo bean?

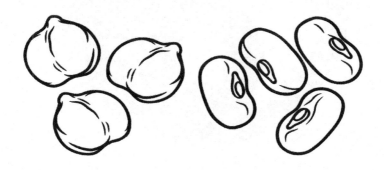

I wouldn't pay $50 to have a garbanzo bean on my face.

What is 6.9?

A good thing
ruined by a
period.

Printed in Great Britain
by Amazon

38062198R00040